Reader

Reader

Robert Glück

The Lapis Press 1989

The Lapis Press
589 N. Venice Blvd.
Venice CA 90291

Distributed by
Publishers Services
P. O. Box 2510
Novato, CA 94948

ISBN 0-932499-66-X

About the cover: the image is a detail from a mysterious plate
reproduced in *Diableries*, ed. Jac Remise (Paris: Balland, 1978).
Cover design: Les Ferriss. Lettering: Christopher Stinehour.

Contents

for ED AULERICH–SUGAI

Wordsworth

Now my dead uncles are stepping forward.

When I look in the mirror this is what I see:

That young people resemble each other, and my own generalized beauty which I admired so shyly & passionately is passing away. Nose thickening, skin solemnly giving up its resiliency. In my face there is a buried sales representative and also a whole family dinner. More than that, bulging eyes & sharp breath, a rabbity kind of fear I could never have named on my father's face but now can identify on my own. Or my mouth sets in a certain way, the way my mother's mouth sets when her course of action is determined. I have admired her courses of action.

I'm especially sorry to say goodbye to the generalized features of mind & body. How many "breakthroughs" by twenty-year-olds I've admired. It's like standing at the edge of someone's garden enthusing over the summer squash. Wordsworth, when he was twenty-eight, said, "For such loss, I would believe abundant recompense." Wordsworth went down to the beach where he could cry and started crying but a wave came up farther than he thought it would so he had to get up and move. He was saying goodbye to the great meaning Natural History conferred on death. Joggers—me with them—ran by like memento mori. I draw wind through my teeth, ruthless exhilaration.

On the other hand, I agree with his conclusion, for opposite reasons. He's philosophic by default. Yet intense pleasure and sadness belong to me more & more. Anxiety less, and with it that mix of anxiety and desire: promiscuity. Even my climaxes are better, which may not be what Wordsworth ever had in mind for me, but who knows what the Romantics meant by "aching joys"?

This acceptance of my face is not an acceptance of the skull beneath it. Wordsworth pushed his death into a rural fantasyland he was smart enough not to examine too closely. His description is beautiful & soft, like listening to peaches. Mine is deferred to that far shore, Further Analysis. I suppose I will have to use language to manufacture distance as my resemblance to the dead increases and my face looks more & more like the complexity of the world.

Mao

Next, let us consider war.

If those who lead a war,
lack experience of war,
then at the initial stage
they will not understand the profound laws
pertaining to the direction of a specific war.
At the initial stage
they will merely experience
a good deal of fighting and,
what is more, suffer many defeats.

But this experience
(the experience of battles won
and especially of battles lost)
enables them to comprehend
the inner thread of the whole war,
namely, the laws of that specific war,
and understand its strategy and tactics,
and consequently to direct the war
with confidence.

If at such a moment
the command is turned over to an inexperienced person,
that person will have to suffer
a number of defeats (gain experience)
before comprehending
the true laws of war.

Elizabethan

Come my Celia let us.
Youth Age Fair Dust
steal (you in) my parting lips,
musical division.

Penetrate or decorate.
I'm jealous—say yes.
Gazing from my only eyes,
twin brutal finitudes,

logic has one root;
but you just shrink
or walk away
into perpetual night.

Look back, look back.

Wieners

A hospital housekeeper cleaning
an emergency room lifted
a sheet off the body of a car wreck
victim and discovered her husband

Here the psyche's fending off
an incursion by an "other"
The skepticism and questioning
are both consciousness and its

projection, like medieval painting,
a pink patch is a tunic with plenty
of space for the body but no body.
Go and line a pleated skirt.

If you're masturbating twice in a row
and imagination lets you down
you need to pull out all the stops,
think about watersports, I do!

—whiff of ammonia—blank wall that
words (exterior and interior) bounce
against. By taking himself apart
he places his judgment in the world.

Libido's a corny circus clown
makes you laugh but really cry
Schizophrenia's a tongue-cut language
but ours. Good council:

I have never-failing advice to unite the separated. I cause speedy, happy marriages, overcome rivals, lover's quarrels, stumbling blocks and bad luck of all kinds. Restore lost nature.

Look up! Astrology's one approach
to charting out the self
but the sky's too small—still there you are
at dusk, star by star.

Lane is not, however, modeled
after a star. He's a carbon
of the body I was married to.
He's an actor in the sense

that all men are actors. They act
like they love you. No I didn't mean
to say that. I don't want to sound
bitter because I'm not bitter at all.

I tenderly lift you in my arms
and carry you up the temple steps
and toss you over the volcano's rim
Plop! see you in China

Son Lane felt first pang of panic
when pulled emergency cord,
figure with mouth open
reeks like burning clutch

Libido's a dopey circus clown
makes you laugh but wish it'd cease,
bestiality necrophelia & sadism—
Don't (I) beat a dead horse (?)

Somebodies With No Bodies

*Two test-tube embryos orphaned by
millionaire American parents
await a life-or-death decision
in deep-freeze in Australia.*

Yeats

I'm the Cold War's breadbox
and zero beyond this
and a shallow darkness
where there is gnashing
& renting & ashes & dirt
eat digest gurgle gurgle
sincere eyes: hi guys
where the hell am I?

MYTH CHOOSES LEDA

BEE: I feel expansive & let the
feeling go past the braking system
I have in my chest.
                    BOB: If you
fly out the window I won't forget
(else it will be trapped in here)
to bring forth this long sigh—

O Mulberry Tree,
God put his lack of being in me.
I can't last the thought of this.
How is a legend a bee-sting's
throbbing silence?

•

Above, the maples—
my breath swayed like a branch.

A Myth for Judy Grahn to Read

Heracles wrestles Antaeus to the ground; Antaeus springs up restored because the Earth is his mother. Her blackbirds echo in pure transparency to high nightingales who echo back with pungent honey. She spills brooks from upper rocks to water the bay. Zeus (of the broad clouds) is Heracles' father. Heracles tames or butchers the symbolic livestock of the local religions of Greece, Italy, Spain and Asia Minor—I'm describing the end of the world again. He kills Hippolyta; Hera hates him; Zeus punishes him: Heracles, you will become a woman's slave, condemned to dress like a woman, spin and weave.

Heracles and Antaeus are well matched (flower of lovely youth, dazzling unmixed light) but Heracles has mastered the new game plan, mobility. He lifts Antaeus away from the earth where long ago there was a city—one arm around Antaeus' ass, the other circling his waist. Antaeus' groin presses its full weight against Heracles' expanding chest. Antaeus arcs backwards, his vision scatters, he smells blood. One hand grapples with Heracles' head, the other rests tenderly on the hero's shoulder.

As I render it, the struggle has an erotic charge. There's not much difference between Heracles and a boa focusing. That's the kind of face a victor is likely to wear.

I'm sorry Antaeus—

Attention slackens and spreads outward; he's an object rather than a subject. He learns how confining life is, now that the borders of his own are broken and invaded. Ribs, spine, pelvis, each gradated second he asks: Can I suffer this much pain and not die? Finally a dark smudge flies out of his mouth, his last breath.

Cavafy

A man loved a man and desired him
the first week the first two months
and also seven years. When his lover
became ill he desired translucence
and the small marks of blood.
In health he desired health.

Torch Song for
Bright-in-Fame Luck to Read

If mountains should
speak my language,
stars crumble, fall
and feel me this radiant

decay. Short Tight Tiny Skirt,
say my name is eternity:
Mr. Motive, Miss Locket,
Mr. Jacket.

Say you want me,
strangers in many ways.
From fetus to antithesis
name me in the dark.

Henri Clouzot

It was not by infidelity that she felt betrayed. She had as many and they amounted to so small an acre in her interior landscape that she assumed the same must be true for him. She looked around at all the Desdemonas & Othellos and laughed. She participated in orgies—they were either fun or not fun. She had sex with strangers—fun or embarrassing. She thought the word betrayal in inverted commas, although he betrayed her constantly, she knew, by his blanket lack of interest in her life. His face looked like so many hands taking, so that after she asked & found out all about him he considered the experience complete & turned away.

•

We were talking (he drops a thrilling octave) *of love*:

Lyric Intermezzo

It was it was two thousand
Rusty years ago and not
A day more when hand in hand
We strolled. It was hot.

Flames of red asters! He lied.
My head grew big as an ice-
Box (Here ends) & down I laid
It. (the pageant of the universe.)

•

Yes, she thinks, Rhys is the flip-side of Austen because it's always money, isn't it? I never thought that was enough for something to be about, money the lubricator. What stands between me & my better self is 10,000 a year plus. And I love the phrase "he has his own money" more than the music of the European meadowlark, didn't Austen?

Sometimes she imagines murdering him at his own depth—other times asking him over to dinner. "Can I have 100 francs?" She hadn't planned to know it would come out so bluntly. Her hand lays derelict on the hero's shoulder.

∙

Interior landscape: his family looking down from the edge of Yosemite Valley, from the edge of the Grand Canyon, King's Canyon, Bryce Canyon, from the Four Corners Monument, from Hoover Dam, at the cliffs of Big Sur, from Niagara Falls, Rainbow Falls, Nevada Falls, his family looking down from the Great Divide.

∙

BORING YOU THINK IT'S BORING? IT'S WHAT PEOPLE KILL EACH OTHER ABOUT!

She looked up at the knife with renewed interest. Sitting at her desk she seemed immensely remote—seemed to recede & the white walls of the room bowled out to receive her. Still she remained *against* him, belittling him by her attitude. She was departing. He interpreted her distance as physical and started after her.

∙

He thinks of a sexual movement a moment—
He slipped into the shower & turned his eyes away from her afraid to get erect & discovered, but the oblique was more suggestive—hailed him deeper—& he had time—only had time—to look back once—directly—before coming—not even getting hard just his head lolling to one side for an instant—

13

A Century for Fredric Jameson to Read

When they came to the great pyramid, they were astonished at the extent of the base, and the height of the top. Imlac explained to them the principles upon which the pyramidal form was chosen for a fabrick intended to co-extend its duration with that of the world: he showed that its gradual diminution gave it such stability as defeated all common attacks of the elements, and could scarcely be overthrown by earthquakes themselves, the least resistible of natural violence. A concussion that should shatter the pyramid would threaten the dissolution of the continent.

Hitler

First they counted on the stupidity of their adversary, and then, when there was no other way out, they themselves simply played stupid. If all this didn't help, they pretended not to understand, or, if challenged, they changed the subject in a hurry, quoted platitudes which, if you accepted them, they immediately related to entirely different matters, and then, if again attacked, gave ground and pretended not to know exactly what you were talking about. Whenever you tried to attack one of these apostles, your hand closed on a jelly-like slime which divided up and poured through your fingers, but in the next moment collected again. But if you really struck one of these fellows so telling a blow that, observed by the audience, he couldn't help but agree, and if you believed that this had taken you at least one step forward, your amazement was great the next day. The Jew had not the slightest recollection of the day before, he rattled off his same old nonsense as though nothing at all had happened, and, if indignantly challenged, affected amazement; he couldn't remember a thing, except that he had proved the correctness of his assertions the previous day.

Sometimes I stood there thunderstruck.

Hitler is a wild exasperation he will transcend by proclaiming "the victory of the idea of creative work, which as such always has been and always will be anti-Semitic." The words of the Jews, the works of Hitler. Hitler sets an equal sign between anti-Semitism and creativity— the camps aren't punishments, they are Parthenons. For the first time I think I understand—I never could from the faces in my family album.

D. Bellamy

Ed sucking me at the baths, everyone looking, scraped my nipple, hey watch out, then pounded my heart once with his fist. I kiddingly leaned back as if stunned but actually found myself fainting till I blacked out & into a rising and welling & dared myself to follow it though I might be dying & felt reckless & struggled higher into the tumult & roaring thinking at the same time the headline in tomorrow's paper would be about me and sordid. I look down—I'm floating—Ed still sucks the cock of my fainted self, I'm held by this, my cock about 15 feet long & knotted in places & I bob at the end. "Now I am totally alienated from my body. This might be a good time to stop and think." In the distance of my distant tip a frail star of sensual feeling.

FO'H

It's so dark today the sky feels like a room
and the room feels like a refrigerator crate
to play in. You have to keep
the light on if you want to read.
And for the welling and serious mounting
of what everything could be
and for the person who reads one page too many
just lie back and watch the light glow
like the moon in daytime.

Pasolini

1

2 crows walk down the road.
One says, "Brother, when the state
is truly communist & out of
the jeweled grasp of church & capital
where even the weeds are looking for a better cemetery,
brother, then we will see—"
Every haystack trembles for the body.
These birds talk good sense. Later they are eaten &
their bones deliciously picked clean.

2

2 crows: politics: to believe and believe.
They experiment, one lies & the other believes,
obvious lies & obvious faith.
What's left stands on one scaly foot,
its head under its wing
and a wink of complicity from the state.

3

2 crows, 2 crows walk down a road
that was shattered by economics.
One crow says "Brother,
I don't know how to make a living.
When I wake up in the morning
tears already stand in my eyes
ready to flow. Brother,
to live in the world,
to change the world."

4

2 crows walk & talk on the desolate
theme of early death.
"Yet lest we may be too one-sided, brother,
notice with what beauty & justice
the sun rises, colors
reflect off their objects, muscles flex,
breath is accepted & enjoyed."

Zero Degree

I dreamt that Kathleen takes me South to this beautiful small town of Maybeck houses & stable elderly people. We give a scheduled poetry reading. Kathleen reads but I've lost my book of poems—tip o' the hat to Freud—and my various places to look yield fragments. Finally I find something I'd been carrying but had forgotten, a long strand of big orange papier-mâché birds, each one different. I tell the audience this is a love poem that I made and I explain each bird's attitude towards love.

•

Seven hours earlier Kathleen lifted a heavy sizzling lid. The chicken, orangy & pink & hopelessly tender, nestled in a nest of carrots & leeks. I said, "It looks like more than itself." I was filled with the sweetness of civilized pleasure and with feelings of reconciliation to a borrowed European childhood that began as a nativity scene under a tree.

•

Beside this sunset pleasure, that is, the pleasure of contemplating a myth, is sensation, the rising sun. When I described someone's orgasm Ed asked, urgent, did his body arch? Another time I said I got dog shit on my finger and he asked, did you smell it? Of course I did and his body had arched.

At the museum: El Greco's *John the Baptist*—ankles like horsehocks, sensual, and light grazing the nipple & running a line between shoulders & head over the clavicle & throat as though the viewer were light touching.

•

Steps for two: The actor who represented X was instructed to take pride in the complexity of his personality. He felt it radiated from an essence which was only his, a negative point that could not be added or subtracted or appraised, so his real life always happened elsewhere. Y's actor was instructed to feel the same about himself except for him this nugget had been crushed, it lay in the dirt and looked like dirt. As destroyed as he felt, he was also proud.

•

I was separating from my lover and had dreams of intense tenderness between us. In these dreams our positions remained pinpoint & oppositional, yet our physical agreement was so large it created an expansive area of reconciliation. Also sometimes, say at a party, I hoped he would do well & succeed, waves of urgency disconnected from the situation. I was nothing beyond that. I described myself complacently as a chicken with its head cut, legs twitching from old neural habits.

•

Last summer something washed up crooked. The wave withdrew and I felt the intensity of seeing what had died. It was an egret; it had strangled on a fish still lodged like an arrow in its bill. I thought I'd appropriate that death one day. I thought I'd use it in a narration which is, Barthes says, "the ideal instrument for every creation of a world." Such a skinny neck. Such a big fish.

K. Fraser

Just a second (face screwed up)

Do you happen to have a window in your house
that someone could talk to a person standing outside of
from and the other person in the house
not hear?

One arm 'round a rosy thigh
in the touched minute.

O what does it matter—
a life is out the window
and you are pulled through.

Violette LeDuc

Only with intimate friends or lots of courage do you forget the French desire to have your complaints canonized. With lesser friends you package complaints as general observations—personality, society—mild revelations adults share like a bundt-cake: sound in structure with a minimum of fantasy, and to be delected, consumed not exactly as nourishment though extrapolated from the idea of nourishment.

I attend a family dinner. When can you call it nourishment and at what point does it become the opposite? My third cousin once removed introduces James Earl Ray to me as a man of profound decadence. I urgently confide the meanest, most shameful details of my life. Ray smiles vacantly across the yellow snapdragons; his eyes do the fox-trot. He tells me that my great-great-grandfather nourished a vampire that annealed to him for three days. His vampire was also called James Earl Ray, and I wonder how that could be a Jewish name? My great-great-grandfather was a rector and refused once to listen (their only hope) to the women's sins.

His daughter had a lady vampire, Lyrical Horror, and after the rector died she desecrated his old photo by having sex with her sister in front of it, pink phlox and purple cineraria. Every character wants to touch a certain other character intimately and for neither of them ever to die. I keep asking what relation they are to me, to the living. My great aunt's grandmother's uncle's half-sister by an earlier marriage sweat 19th-century perfume in her brother's bulging arms. Each relation buries me deeper, is above what I can know. He starts to throw water in my confused faced to wake me up, but I protest. "Better to be metaphorical," I say, not sure if that's true about listening to evil, so he just licks his finger and flicks the spit in my ear.

Genre Novel for Dennis Cooper to Read

Quickly he got up, rubbed
The sleep from his eyes.
He grabbed his bathrobe
And headed for the shower   Yes I believed nothing—

Down the hall. He stood
Under the stinging spray
And lathered suds into the
Hardened planes of his body.   now the eclipse is a face

Finally he shut off
The hot water and
Cringed beneath the shock
Of the ice-cold deluge.   like L.A. where air is

He let his breath out slowly,
Relaxing his swollen muscles,
And shut off the spray.
He stood shivering, water   emotion. There was a cry

Dripping upon the tiles
From the shiny wetness
Of his nude flesh. He
Grabbed for the towel,   of tortured agony.

Ruffled it through his tawny hair,
Over the rounded firmness of his
Shoulders and tobogganed the rough
Terrycloth down the rugged columns   The knife rose quick

Of his legs. He punished
His rugged body
Brutally until
His skin was alive   as a serpent's tongue

And glowing with masculine
Beauty and good health.
The body that was
Reflected in the oval   slicing across Ian's

Mirror was the picture
Of masculine perfection,
A body cast in the poetical
Imagery of Byron   features. The mind dreams

Or the bronze sculpture
Of Rodin. . . . The air
Was electric with deep
And meaningful emotion.   to prevent boredom.

Learning to Write / Basho

family   as-for

all   staff-with   leaning   white-hair

go   grave-visiting

$$3 \quad 2$$

$$1 \quad 2 \quad 2 \quad 2$$

$$1 \quad 4$$

A visit to the family graves in my native village in remembrance of the recent death of my common-law wife. There are present (in addition to myself) my wife's mother, my two older brothers and their wives, and also my wife's brother. My two daughters are still in Edo. The "family" is small and certainly made up of elderly people. My oldest brother has no children, and my second brother's oldest son, whom I had adopted, died within the year. I'm already looking forward to my own death and, on this occasion, it seems to me, looking forward to the probable extinction of my whole family as well.

Hokusai's *Manga*

*A samurai tracks through woods watched by the supernatural, which he knows
(tiles of carp-scale, cormorant feathers for thatch) but momentarily forgets.
Struggle between ancient houses, ridicule, confusion:*

A warrior bragged about his strength; finally he was summoned to a
wrestling tournament. He rode through a maple forest of "burning
leaves" where he caught a glimpse of an attractive woman dressed in
indigo cloth and carrying a bucket of water on her head. The woman
was thinking about clumsiness, about a maidservant who dropped one
of a set of ten treasured porcelain bowls decorated with long-haired
turtles in gold and silver lusters. The master berated her so severely that
she jumped into an old well where, from that night, you could hear her
hollow voice counting and re-counting the remaining dishes. The war-
rior dismounted and caught the woman's hand. The woman didn't
resist but said dreamily, eyes on the distance, "—or if it rains from a
low cloud, or if a shadow half-covers a valley, or a lagoon, or if it doesn't,
or if a tree branch looks particularly attractive in itself, surely not
because it resembles an elephant's gray leg. . . ."

The warrior sees this as
encouragement. He gently takes her arm and the woman releases her
hold on the bucket and clamps his wrist under her armpit with such
force that a line of cranes whizzes past the couple and nature divides in
front of them and rejoins behind. The warrior tries to escape; he
digs in his heels and ripples his muscles but he can't pull free, and the
woman marches serenely on. The warrior isn't the first to fall in love
with a dead person or to misjudge the power of his beloved—to mis-
judge the origin of her strength. No wonder he's outclassed. We can
have no idea of how many ghosts there are or how many people love
them; they seem irresistible to a certain type who hungers for excel-
lence.

She's thinking about revenge, about a cousin who was born ugly because her mother drowned the cousin's half-sister by an earlier marriage. The cousin inherited an acre by the river, so a peasant married and then murdered her. For years she haunted the riverside, driving the peasant's subsequent wives to their deaths.

Now the warrior pleads to be set free, says he's due at a wrestling match. The woman laughs. "I have a little story to tell you. A giant said, 'Nothing can fell me.' A hero replied, 'A little thing can fell you.' The hero dashed forward and drove a pick through the giant's little toe. The giant roared, transmuted pain into rage and scooped up the hero who said, 'Now I'm going to rent a room at the corner of Hell Street and I shall be happy to see you whenever you pass by.' The giant tore him in half the long way and threw both pieces up so high they disappeared. It was a stunning victory for giants and monsters."

Earlier, the warrior felt he had mastered the subject of death. Soon she will teach him that once you master a subject the subject masters you. Later the warrior will locate under every smell the sweet pointed decadence, even though the leaves are on their trees. Now they embark on a relationship in which every intimacy is rejected; her bucket will not spill even a drop. The warrior still doesn't know she's a ghost; if he could glance down he'd see that she has no feet. "You! Wrestling! Live with me for three weeks—I'll toughen you up!"

A Ballad for
Kevin Killian to Read

I seldom look at my ears
so when I do
they're strangers

I seldom even look at my eyes
when I do
I love them

my nose
stranger

mouth
loooove

a car smashes a dog barks
O strangers in the night

Shakespeare

Night is black space
Day so warm and blue it hangs against my face,

says Edmund who knows more than Gloucester.
That "more than" structures Time,
Time slays the parting guest
and welcomes you up on a school or battlement,
"Take a few classes, take
a prerequisite. . . ."

Behind, the past; above, the skies;
A self is more credible if it dies,

says Iago, a Cookie
who can't imagine the stove.
He cries, What use these ceremonies to you?
Next room: secrets known,
happenstance is
luminous, inclusive. . . .

Next room: The dead propose to make you deader,
They teach you one thing, then another.
Alternately: That's a hazard to the reader.

In other words, read this over your dead body,
said Shakespeare

Faith says, and adds

Form is the occasion (funeral or birthday)
To give the body away.

Faith decks out your skeleton in the bilateral poetry of perception and motion. Between these discernments, eyes, ears, arms and legs, Faith runs a line of disruption and abundance, Acker, Ahab, Watten, Oz. . . .

It's more complex than I expect
Too bad it isn't more complex.

a b a b c d c
d e f e f g g

WWII

In a specific type of discourse on sex, in a specific form of extortion of truth, appearing historically and in specific places . . . what were the most immediate, the most local power relations at work?

"I have become extremely flighty and very easily upset. I can't control some of the things I say, and I find myself involuntarily giving myself away. Each time someone new learns, I am thrown into a frenzy, for soon it will be utterly unbearable and I shall have to turn to anything I can find, to get away from here before everyone knows, and I become a complete outcast."

THE GAG REFLEX AND FELLATIO

This observation, first made at an induction station in 1942, was studied further in 1,404 patients at a neuropsychiatric military hospital in 1944. The gag reflex evaluation was made in each case. It was tested by manipulating a tongue depressor around the uvula, soft palate, and pharyngeal vault. Normally the stimulus innervates the 9th and 10th cranial nerves supplying this area and produces the gag reflex. In subjects practicing fellatio this reflex is absent even when the tongue depressor is inserted well into the vault of the pharynx.

		%
1. Constitutional psychopathic state:		
(a)	Sexual psychopathology, fellatio	89
(b)	Drug addiction	36
2. Psychoneurosis, hysteria		50
3. Schizophrenia		18

The test was also used during the past two years in a civilian hospital. As in the above report, here too the findings were very satisfying.

How did they make possible these kinds of discourses,

QUESTION: Do you wish to sleep with your mother?

ANSWER: No. I have no desire for that (pause of several seconds) . . . but why not? . . . I have too much pride for that . . . she never asked me to—

The private letters and medical essays (from the *American Journal of Psychiatry* and the *Journal of Abnormal and Social Psychology*) are part of Allan Bérubé's research on gays in World War II; the topic sentences are from Foucault's *History of Sexuality*.

In conclusion, it is felt the test is a definite aid in screening candidates not only for the military services but for positions where the sexual deviant must be eliminated.

and conversely, how were these discourses used to support power relations?

"This morning I saw the psychiatrist. I went in his office and after a few routine questions he asked me to stand up in front of him—he had me pull my shirt up and my pants down. He starts running his hands around my back and chest and slowly working his way down to the inevitable—he asked me to say whatever came into my mind—but after he went through this routine we settled down to the $64 question."

Freud was the first to emphasize the close association between homosexuality and paranoia. In the Armed Services this relationship is frequently seen.

How was the action of these power relations modified by their very exercise . . . so that there has never existed one type of subjugation, given once and for all?

"The last terrible barrier between us is down and I am revealed shame-faced and defiant in all my abnormality and cowardice. Don't be too severe with me, please understand how heartbreaking it is for me to write such a letter. I feel that I have disgraced you, betrayed you in the worst possible way. . . ."

"All of your present friends are loyal to you, for *you*, as is, and don't assume a cringing attitude. I hope that you have opened up the way to a more honest relationship with pa and me."

"Sometimes I think our lives will always be hell. You can't blame it on the army."

How were these relations linked to one another according to the logic of a great strategy, which in retrospect takes on a unitary and volunteerist politics of sex?

"When I entered the army I had certain homosexual tendencies. Army life has developed them into traits of character which I will never be able to change."

"Frisco was absolutely beyond recall. I have never seen a thing like it—everywhere, anything on Powell Street—*anything* on *any* street. . . ."

"You can't blame it on the Army—it's the whole damn world and we were just born at the wrong time—all we want is to love and to express what is in our souls and thank God we have something to express. How-ever, we must remain friends and someday, God knows when, but some-day we can help each other."

D. H. Lawrence

Stanley felt empty:
life has no meaning.
He looked frightened.
We tried to cheer him up,
agreeing with him
or predicting he was wrong.

Stanley left for home
but stopped at Fifes.
We'd had some grass
and three beers and
now he ordered another
and another.

Any man, any man floated over
on the slightest inclination
of Stanley's head—
then the Groundskeeper.
Stanley admired his spirit
and he spent the night
in the Groundskeeper's cabin
with its cot, its cat
and herb garden.

Next morning I met Stanley
for breakfast. He related
the story and added
that he felt a lot better.
He looked better.

When we were convincing
Stanley, Giuliano, Stanley's
lover, suggested love.
I think love
is a temporary measure
but I know Stanley's fear
by desiring its cure.

R. Duncan

The schemer encloses his desire in a riddle;
his first voice is the knock-knock joke's—
his other cultivates disorder.

Cultivation and disorder
haunt the room I live in.
I am speaking of a threshold,

a ghost
who raps you on the head with a question—
who's there?
That breed of interruption is always a new joke.
Where

is the fancy bred?
How   is it read? Where
does it lie? Apple of the void behind my eye,
reply, reply.

Keats

Darkling you listened;
   and, for many a time
you had been half in love
   with easeful Death,
called him soft names
   in many a muséd rhyme
to take into the air
   your quiet breath—

From my bedroom window
   I see the belly
of a small plane
   light up with sun.
Remember my father—
   chocolate kisses
from on high,
   flags and nuggets
of silver foil.
   Afternoon. People waft,
breezes in Paradise.
   We are sentimental
in my kitchen; on TV
   Baryshnikov does
everything the body can.
   Don't think about dying—
how is a grand jeté
   cut flowers in a glass.
Sharon glided to death
   on the freeway.
She was younger
   than I am now.

I start awake—
    wind or heartbeat
shakes the house—
    it's 4 a.m.—

Ovid

—therefore I am
a tree. Blue patches
drift between
my lazy fingers,

in the hot sun
a cool breeze.

Mom, help me.
Up to my neck
in your body
I'm so lonesome
it could die—

a cool cemetery
breeze, I've
always been away,

always just returned
unappeased
by opposites, kinships,
and I think

therefore I am
a tree. Blue patches
drift between
my lazy fingers,

in the hot sun
a cool breeze.

Bataille

World before, world after:
Credo.   visible
Curtain: Let the hidden   be quicksand
Be visible.

Everything in the dark
Wanted,   sightsee through
Everyone in the back   parted lids
Wanted the front.

Lechers fell in unison—
Body   become dream
Of a rose about to go.   substances
Child substances:

Scab, spit, rust, mercury.
Mom & dad   Comte Dona-
So small from up here, big   tien Alphonse
From down here, inside-

Out, honk if you agree
Tourist,   François
Pushed from your own lip,   de Sade
Eager to fall.

A Government for Bruce Boone to Read

To choose a profession each adult must afford the government a piece of his parent's body, the piece depending on the profession. A male gives from his mother's or grandmother's body, a female gives from her father's or grandfather's. For instance, if a man wants to be a lawyer he furnishes the eye-teeth of his mother or grandmother. The man or woman must yield a more substantial section for employment less beneficial to the community, an example of government channeling. The woman who decides to be indigent must part with her father's legs.

Fashion responded, the flat-chested look, designers and movie stars. Style-conscious parents sever their breasts to show baby will be a doctor. A considerable number did this never supposing the details of the body-assignment law would change. When they did change, people had their first inkling that the government was against them.

The 50s for James Purdy to Read

bring them to the brink of consummation
force them to retreat
bring them to the brink of consummation
take them off the heat
bring them to the brink of consummation
inflict shame and doubt
Gay bar—gaze down
from heaven—hellish gleam.
Irresistible the obsessive coiling—
moral nature—snakes in a pit.
Wife, yolk and white, continue the species.

One: feels so much so deeply:
hangs himself his tongue bulging
in mockery of *and* shoots himself
the barrel in mouth a mockery of
and knifes himself the penetration
drowns himself ocean little homeless
sperm—skull glees from headless
Death's crotch. The friend
recoils from his friend, then recoils
it was a bad dream, then in horror
        at the dreamer—

"CRUEL, RELENTLESS . . . The Nightmare extremes
of the homosexual experience . . . Fully exposed down
to its rawest nerve endings." *Newsweek*

"It describes brutalities too raw for paraphrase . . . . It
is cruel and clinical, yet tender. It ends in death; it ends
in hope." *Los Angeles Times*

Mallarmé

Aunt Inez, Uncle Baffle. He was beautifully stuck in the ice and ruffled his primaries disdainfully to indicate the life of the mind. These were beautiful intentions, but much in the way of communication was beneath them. Aunt Inez quoted his gesture, substituting golden tresses for wing feathers and her mind for his. How tired she was (he made her) of every single curlicue. . . .

I *hate* these ringlets,
I *hate* them!
Aunt Inez is played
by Peter Lorre.
Another Inez turns
to a slightly different me:
That's a cheap shot.
And sexist. Why
was I always relegated?
Didn't I practically
write his dissertation?

A third Inez turns:
Sexist. Polite deferral
into suspended animation.

Inez gets in the car.
Inez,
she gets in her car
and makes the long drive home.

I wish he wouldn't always
want to go ice-skating
in bed, but is there enough
wrong for one of us to say,
out loud, what's wrong?

Years later she answered herself:
    He put his lack of being on me without benefit of clergy.
    I'm not the local color for his or anyone's psyche.
    I left him that night in as many ways as a person can.
    It was ages since I'd felt so light and frisky.

Burroughs

flashes his dirty rotten hunka tin   I am right   strapped into head
electrodes   he sticks a gun in teen age drug   Harry S. Truman de-
cided to drop first   I am right   sequence   repeat   dim jerky far away
smoke   cop rat bares his yellow teet   kicks in the door   I am right
survivors burned   time and place   he throws atom bomb   knocks
man to floor   you are wrong   you are wrong   he was looking for are
wrong   Breaks through door Im poli   outside bar   Hiroshima   has
strayed into Dillinger's right   is making a difficult decision   right
survivors burned   mixed you child I am   he kicks him into 1914 movie
if you are gay I am right   wrong   executioner   officer   I am cop
right enough you are I am right   right   wrong   Pentagon   dim
jerky far away smoke.

I cut up his cut-ups, allegory of an allegory of an allegory of an allegory
of a waterfall of mental curlicues whose new meaning is no meaning in
extremity. Is a Burroughs to eat? I am timid, abstract, complete, light
fever, timid. Barefoot, yells Hey Pop, got any more Dick Tracys?
Burroughs am paying one wrecked penny for the pleasure he's wreaking
on some "boy"; shooting quarts of toxins, skin a welcome mat, body
heroically disjunct Picasso (two profiles, left front thigh . . .) The
stapled urge for self-protection that. . . . Danger is a refuge from more
danger. Don't even know what a Burroughs is.

Manhattan Project, first atom bomb test, New Mexico 1945: Oppen-
heimer and *his* boys think the planet could go critical. Oppenheimer re-
figures, the probability remains, "What the hell." So-and-so many
blasts: radioactive sex causes untold genetic mutations. A carnival of
giants, vile luminosity sheeting off their scales and exoskeletons, march
out of that desert looking for something to eat. I don't want to die but
witness APPETITE and MURDER tread the vile luminous sand:

ant spider Gila monster rattler wasp rat locust lizard grasshopper rabbit praying mantis crow ant spider wasp. . . . The entire town of Soda Bluff stampedes down narrow canyons scattering funeral lights beneath their trembling feet. The destruction of today. Last men, mercenaries on the last patrol, eat rations with dog mouths, then fool around in caustic green dusk; they wear Mylar capes and copper-studded jockstraps. Bud's withheld a basket musta weigh two pounds of fresh peaches. Bud squirms down with a deep sigh, odor of penetration, he says "I want to be so *embraced.*" The last ant cold mandibles his thigh, a howl and spasms from Bud's lifted body mean death. I send my own spear into the enormous insect eye shattering a thousand selves— point touches pinpoint brain, blue sparks, burning isolation, burning rubber, ant collapses, cold heap of old parts. The reason Bud dies, so that his orgasm stays beyond. I don't wonder *who* I am, I wonder *where* I am—still, nothing to do now but kick back and wait for orders.

The Iliad

help me—I am Bob's cry for help.

O—I am Bob's shield.

A Movie for John Karr to Read

INTRODUCTION

that they actually remove their they couldn't
remove their, no no they couldn't unbuckle unbutton
drop—impossible, impossible from dressed to
naked chasm abyss idiocy of the future—easier to
throw back head and bare teeth till incisors grow
skeleton is gleaming ruined than reveal no
they couldn't reveal easier to die than take off
take off jockey shorts than push my, easier to die
than spurt cities in space, legs spread impossible

EXPOSITION

Let me introduce you to the rest of the staff
They turn out to be cocks
A pink tourist inchworms along the blue baseboard

Miss Cock this is Mr. Cock
Pleased to meet you
     For liberation
Likewise I'm sure
     Break an old taboo
Mrs. Cock this is
Mrs. Cock?
She's a widow
     For a new civilization
obsess obsess
Mr. Cock you're exuding
     Make a new taboo
takes out a handkerchief
     subliminal message
dab dab dab

CLOSE-UPS

life jacket: yo! mom and dad and their big oaf
in their red canoe want to know
how they are unique and want to know
how same in the community of standing
touching where pleasure is how
unique and same and unique—

mud: is also a place on the map and radar screen's
barely enough and always too much to believe in

pendulum: still we want to see a tip reach
excruciation and singleness
then fall back (I die)
abundance and wealth
of falling back

erection: want to gaze at an eclair tasting itself

family outing:

we pass an upper window where—

we see into a window—

The Chronicle

1

A swank luncheon thrown in Union Square by San Francisco society's premiere hostess broke up today with apple cores & curses & police drawing guns.

2

It was a catered affair featuring white-gloved waiters, staged by Charlotte Mailliard (pronounced Mā-yard) in honor of I. Magnin exec. John Brunelle. A section of the square was cordoned off & decorated with pastel balloons.

3

A bar was set up & drinks began pouring by noon. These events excited considerable interest in onlookers, which deepened as 40 guests sat down to spoon up their vichyssoise, wash it down with chilled Pinot Blanc & proceed to their avocados stuffed with shrimp.

4

90 minutes: murmurings turned to jeers: Rich Pigs Go Home. Psychiatrist Richard Kunin, laying his napkin down, rose to his feet & sought to reason.

5

"I told them, 'It can be painful being on the outside looking in.' I said, 'I've been there before and I suppose I will again.' " And by extension will they dine one day at the table of Charlotte Mailliard? In this way he bribed them with the distant mansions of country-western music.

Dr. Kunin functions as the mediating ideologue. He belongs to the echelon that works for its betters by creating imaginary resolutions of real contradictions. (For ex., Charlotte Mailliard remained blandly intact, said, "They were the entertainment.")

6

Jeers resumed & drowned out the music. The guests uneasily swallowed their long-stemmed strawberries. "We didn't want to lose face in front of the enemy."

7

When patrolmen Walsh & Scott arrived the first apple cores were flying and the air was blue and red with curses and rhetoric. They pulled their guns and shouldered their way, politely saying, "Excuse me, excuse me."

8

By this time the waiters were assembling the silver in some haste. Charlotte Mailliard, who this week gave a party for dogs, said Brunelle always wanted to eat lunch there & never got the chance.

Personal Reflection

More interesting than her character is the question: What forces generate interior landscapes of blackmail & cocktail parties for dogs? When asked her view by the press the rich rich rich Charlotte Mailliard answered, "I give more than I've received."

9

Three men were arrested. Two escaped. Nabbed: Richard Sawyer, 26, unemployed truck driver from Susanville. He called the *Chronicle* from City Prison. "I was just walking through the park & saw all the people & the balloons & the police grabbed hold of me."

Jack Spicer

THE SCREEN	THE AUDIENCE
when wind she blows	Will Jennifer Jones
	either to her mirror
from Africa	US family and not
	faceless in Infidelity
I'll beata you	dote on her Italian lover
	Montgomery Clift
don think abouta	*dote on him* doubt
	is a wound that leaks self
thata green white &	Aphrodite doesn't promise
	happiness but smut
red flag-faced nuns	and trouble.
signal shock, sleezy hobo	
sly libido, nephew	
	A lively silence, a crude sulk,
normal, flashbulbs	an itch asserts
	my novel my trip my health my . . .
I am nothing beyond this	
—Sunday! the tone	
knows more than they,	Say faith hops a freight
	image by image by image by . . .
ideal bell.	whose light means, well, light.

There's no question in my mind except
when he looks at me. Harry, little Heidi,
cupcake of the Cold War, her thirty Heidi
suits of steel and tin. . . .

I surround Montgomery Clift with my body,
no thought to heal him, I require
his wound and rightly to deal our sex
a little death unknown in Philadelphia,
bland Valhalla. But soon I'm shrilling
stand up straight to make the crumpled
desert bloom.
Like you the train with its utterly alien cargo
moves on the black track—
The Goodbye Forever Limited pants, well, *goodbye*
as my skin retreats in an uproar.
Like you like you I do what the future wants.

Kafka

What says the WICKED SON?
—"Of what use is this ceremony to you?" *To you*, and not to himself! By excluding himself from the community, he has denied the Deity. Do thou, then, set his teeth on edge! Say to him: "This is on account of what the Lord did *for me* when *I* went forth from Egypt." *For me*, and not for him; had he been there, he would not have been redeemed.

Henry James

Our skull cancels biography and we gape at
    the height of the arch and extent of its
    base. Under my face the little Dog
    laughs at individual life,

at the stress that stemware & flatware are
    nothing beyond this. But seizing the
    inner thread of the dinner party:

then the dish tells the spoon a beautiful
    ugly story, structural loneliness
    pertaining to the direction of grueling
    border wars. We pool our gestures
    though much in the way of comparison
    is beyond us

except the older soprano's moon flight
    raised like a Hymn, not lowered like
    a Shade, Eurydice lifting the dome's
    massed clouds and soft soil: These
    Fields of sweet repose/this happy
    domicile/of final Good—

hear in your head. Now baby resembles.
He'll get our brainy eyes and hollow skull.

Poetry

Any fear
asserts body
and its eyes widen.
Any body, asserted,
wants consummation
"to the height
of this great argument."
Here's the brink,
the smile, the camera,
the few steps back—

Sl—p is autumn:
When others are
Sleepy my eyes
Weep. M—ney
Is a peaked cap:
Under it multitudes
Though we are one.
P—try is exaggerated
History: That's my
Last Duchess as if
Alive. D—th
Sublime: I shall
Not want for nothing.
L—st the forger:
On an unmade bed
I shall not want.

My itsy-bitsy body
climbs up its spout.
My voice makes noises
to cast distance out.
The noise makes words
which let distance in.
My unmade body
is made again.

Acknowledgements

Versions of the writing in this collection appeared under the working title *Learning to Write*; some were published in the following magazines & journals: *New Directions Anthology, City Lights Journal, Northern Literary Quarterly, Ironwood, Acts, Jimmy & Lucy's House of "K," The Sentinel, Noe Valley Voice, Transfer, Mirage, Fire in the Lake, No Apologies, Soup, Stanford Journal of Italian Studies, Social Text, Semiotext(e)*, and the anthologies *Storyteller* and *An Ear to the Ground*.

Reader was designed by Les Ferriss and set in Monotype Van Dijck by Mackenzie-Harris Corp. in San Francisco. Printed by Les Ferriss and Eric A. Johnson at The Lapis Press Studio, Emeryville, California. The paper is acid-free Mohawk Superfine. 1000 copies bound by Cardoza-James in San Francisco.